D0688164

FOOTBALL'S
BEST
AND
WORST

A Guide to the Game's
Good, Bad, and Ugly

by
DREW LYON

CAPSTONE PRESS
a capstone imprint

Sports Illustrated Kids Best and Worst of Sports are published by Capstone Press, 1710 Roe Crest Drive, North Mankato, Minnesota 56003
www.mycapstone.com

Library of Congress Cataloging-in-Publication data

Names: Lyon, Drew, author.
Title: Football's best and worst : a guide to the game's good, bad, and ugly / by Drew Lyon.
Description: North Mankato, Minnesota : Capstone Press, 2018. | Series: Sports illustrated kids. The best and worst of sports | Audience: Age 9-14.
Identifiers: LCCN 2017047196 (print) | LCCN 2017048695 (ebook) | ISBN: 9781543506228 (eBook PDF) | ISBN: 9781543506143 (hardcover)
Subjects: LCSH: Football — Miscellanea — Juvenile literature.
Classification: LCC GV950.7 (ebook) | LCC GV950.7 .L96 2018 (print) | DDC 796.332 — dc23
LC record available at https://lccn.loc.gov/2017047196

Editorial Credits

Nate LeBoutillier, editor; Bob Lentz and Terri Poburka, designers; Eric Gohl, media researcher; Laura Manthe, production specialist

Photo Credits

AP Photo: San Francisco Examiner, 11; Dreamstime: Scott Anderson, 25; Getty Images: Bettmann, 16, Focus On Sport, 5, 19 (top), New York Daily News, 9, Rob Brown, 17, Sports Illustrated/John Iacono, 18, Stringer/Jamal Wilson, 27 (bottom); Newscom: Cal Sport Media/Jason Pohuski, 29 (bottom left), Icon Sportswire/John Cordes, 21, Icon Sportswire/Rich Graessle, cover (left), Reuters/Stringer, 14, Reuters/USA Today Sports, 6, SportsChrome/Rob Tringali, cover (right), UPI/Gary C. Caskey, 24, USA Today Sports/Tim Fuller, 12, ZUMA Press/Keith Birmingham, 19 (bottom); Sports Illustrated: Al Tielemans, 7 (top), 28 (bottom), 29 (bottom right), Bill Frakes, 15, Bob Rosato, 10, 13, 20 (bottom), Damian Strohmeyer, 4, 20 (top), David E. Klutho, 28 (top), Heinz Kluetmeier, 7 (bottom), John Biever, 27 (top), John W. McDonough, 26, Peter Read Miller, 8, Robert Beck, 22 (bottom), 23 (all), Simon Bruty, 22 (top), 29 (top)

Printed and bound in the United States of America.
010783S18

TABLE of CONTENTS

Nobody's Perfect
(Except for the 1972 Dolphins)

The tradition has remained for decades. Each season when the last undefeated NFL team loses, members from the 1972 Miami Dolphins gather to celebrate. That's because the '72 Dolphins finished their season 17-0 and stand alone as the lone undefeated team in NFL history.

There have been close calls. After the 2007 New England Patriots won their first 18 games, the '72 Dolphins prepared to make room at the top. But the Patriots lost in the Super Bowl to the underdog New York Giants, ending what had been the Patriots' best season ever with the worst loss in franchise history.

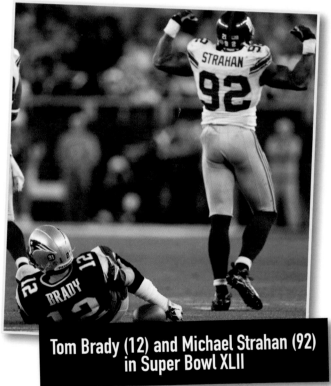

Tom Brady (12) and Michael Strahan (92) in Super Bowl XLII

But that's how it goes in pro football. All-Star players have poor games. Average players have fantastic moments. The league's best linebacker can be a quarterback's worst nightmare. One fan's victory is another fan's loss. One thing is certain: it's all very entertaining.

BEST EVER!

Larry Csonka (39) and Larry Little (66) of the 1972 Miami Dolphins

CHAPTER 1

Playmakers & Heartbreakers

RECEIVERS

Receivers are often the brightest stars of the shows in today's National Football League (NFL). Their acrobatic, gravity-defying catches top the highlight reels. But big drops in key moments can also lead to frustration, finger-pointing, and failure.

It took just one catch for the New York Giants' **Odell Beckham, Jr.** to become a football sensation. The Giants were playing Dallas when quarterback Eli Manning threw a pass from midfield. Beckham sped down the sidelines, but was held by a defender. A penalty flag was thrown while the ball was in the air.

Beckham freed his hands and outstretched his right arm. The end of the football stuck in his paw . . . and Beckham caught the ball with just three fingers! Without letting the ball touch the ground, he hung on to the pigskin and fell backward into the end zone.

"I hope it's not the greatest catch of all time," Beckham later said. "I hope I can make more."

BEST!

ONE-HAND WONDER

Odell Beckham, Jr

SUPER DROP

The New England Patriots were holding a slim lead over the New York Giants late in Super Bowl XLVI in 2012. A couple more first downs and the Pats could drain the clock and ice the game.

On second down, Tom Brady dropped back to pass. He looked to Pro Bowl receiver Wes Welker,

Wes Welker

who was open near the 25-yard line. But Brady's pass was slightly off the mark, forcing Welker to twist to his right. The ball bounced off Welker's hands, and Patriots fans smacked their palms to their foreheads.

"Welker makes that catch a hundred times out of a hundred," commentator Cris Collinsworth said after watching the replay. Um, better make that 99 times out of 100, Cris. Minutes later, the Giants got the ball and won on an amazing last-ditch drive.

EWW!

THAT'S A FACT
Some NFL players once applied an adhesive spray from a can to their hands to help them catch footballs. The spray was called Stickum, which the league officially banned in 1981. Many of today's players wear (legal) gloves that aid in making fantastic catches.

RUNNING BACKS

Handling the pigskin can be risky business. The best running backs carry the ball through heavy contact with the quickest of feet. The best quarterbacks throw it with accuracy and grace. But sometimes . . . the ball doesn't seem cooperate.

#BEASTQUAKE

Marshawn Lynch

BEST!

There's no doubt why Marshawn Lynch's nickname is "Beast Mode." Lynch embraced collisions, which led to a jaw-dropping run in a 2010 playoff game.

Lynch's Seattle Seahawks were trying to fend off the New Orleans Saints late in the fourth quarter when the running back took a handoff from quarterback Matt Hasselbeck. He shook off a Saints tackler, bounced to his right, and broke two more tackles.

Around midfield, he shook off another tackler before giving Saints cornerback Tracy Porter a vicious stiff arm that sent Porter falling backwards. Lynch scampered to the sidelines with his teammates trailing him. With one more Saints defender to beat, Lynch cut left, eluded one last tackle at about the two-yard line, and leaped into the end zone.

The "Beast Quake" was felt all around the league.

THAT'S A FACT
At the relatively young age of 29, Marshawn Lynch retired from football after the 2015 NFL season. He un-retired and came back to play for his hometown Oakland Raiders in 2017.

When New York Jets quarterback Mark Sanchez took the snap, he had no idea the play would end with one of the NFL's most hilarious bloopers.

Sanchez was under center against New England in a game played on Thanksgiving Day, 2012. He turned left after receiving the snap. That was his first mistake — the play call was designed for Sanchez to turn right and hand the ball off to running back Shonn Greene. Unable to connect with Greene, Sanchez ran forward hoping to salvage a few yards. But he ran right into the backside of Brandon Moore, his own right guard. Sanchez's head snapped back and he fumbled the ball, and the Patriots scooped it up and ran it in for a touchdown.

Sanchez's goof was a first-ballot entry into the Blooper Hall of Fame. The "Butt Fumble" won ESPN's "Not Top 10" award for a record 40 straight weeks.

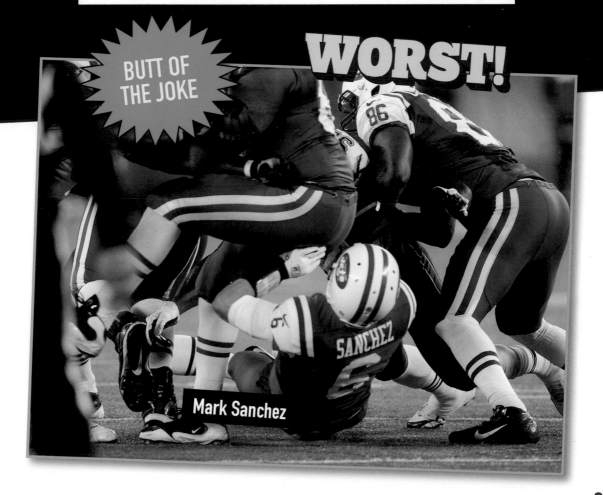

BUTT OF THE JOKE

WORST!

Mark Sanchez

BEST!

WILD PLAYS

The play that's drawn up often doesn't go according to plan. Sometimes magic happens. In other cases, confusion creates bloopers that stand the test of time.

When the Buffalo Bills took a one-point lead with 16 seconds left in the game, the home crowd in Nashville ("Music City") felt deflated.

The Tennessee Titans needed a miracle to win the 1999 AFC Wild Card game when Bills kicker Steve Christie popped up a short kickoff to the 25-yard line. Tennessee's **Lorenzo Neal** received the ball before pitching it to **Frank Wycheck**. He turned to his left and threw to Frank Dyson.

Dyson caught the ball and sprinted forward. He couldn't believe his eyes — there wasn't a Bills player in sight! Dyson sprinted 75 yards to the end zone, but Wycheck's lateral was close to being an illegal forward pass.

After review, the referee ruled there wasn't enough visual evidence to overturn the play. Game over! Titans win!

Jim Marshall was a four-time Pro Bowler for the Minnesota Vikings. But he's remembered among casual NFL fans for running 66 yards in the wrong direction.

In a 1965 game against the San Francisco 49ers, Marshall recovered a fumble. But he somehow got turned around and headed the wrong way, sprinting the into the end zone opposite the one he *should've* been aiming for. By the time Marshall realized his goof, it was too late.

Thinking he'd scored a touchdown, Marshall celebrated by tossing the ball into the stands, thereby giving the 49ers a two-point safety. Luckily for Marshall, he redeemed himself later in the game by causing a key fumble that directly led to a Vikings touchdown and a 27-22 win.

Jim Marshall

CHAPTER 2

Champs & Choke Artists

HOLY HAIL MARY!

QUARTERBACKS

Quarterbacks are football's field generals. The difference between completed passes and interceptions can be razor thin. And when games come down to that final moment, some stars shine brighter than others.

Aaron Rodgers

THAT'S A FACT

Dallas Cowboys quarterback Roger Staubach first coined the desperation pass a "Hail Mary" after throwing a last-second touchdown to Drew Pearson in a 1975 playoff game.

BEST!

Most passers are lucky to complete one last-ditch, game-winning prayer of a touchdown pass in their career. By the age of 33, Green Bay Packers QB **Aaron Rodgers** had already completed three Hail Marys.

Rodgers' first Hail Mary traveled nearly 70 yards in the air and came in 2015, in a last-second win versus the Detroit Lions. That was the longest Hail Mary completion in NFL history. A few games later, Rodgers did it again in the playoffs. This time the opponent was Arizona, and the touchdown pass went for 59 yards. For good measure, Rodgers did it once again in 2016. Again, the stakes were high as the Packers were in the playoffs against the New York Giants. This Hail Mary came before halftime, not at the end of the game. But the "amazing" factor was as sky high as the flight of Rodgers' pass.

A FAVRE-FETCHED FINISH

WORST!

Brett Favre

Brett Favre had more than his fair share of dramatic finishes in his 20-season career as an NFL quarterback. In 2009 Favre was in the twilight of his career and had led the Minnesota Vikings to the NFC title game versus the New Orleans Saints. A victory would mean a berth in the Super Bowl. With 19 seconds left and the score tied at 28, Favre had led the Vikings into field goal range. The idea was to run one more play to gain a few yards and then kick the game-winning field goal.

Instead of trying for a short gain, Favre rolled to his right and threw downfield to his left. It was a daredevil, across-the-body throw that he'd completed just a week earlier. This time, however, Saints cornerback Tracy Porter was ready. He jumped Favre's pass, intercepting it. New Orleans went on to win in overtime, leaving Minnesota devastated.

SUPER BOWLS

Every February, millions of people gather around their televisions to watch the two best football teams determine who will win the Lombardi Trophy. Some games are epic, but every once in awhile, the Super Bowl is a super bore.

Super Bowl LI following the 2016 season seemed like a laugher by halftime. The **Atlanta Falcons** were blowing out the favored New England Patriots 21-3 and added another touchdown to lead 28-3 with 8:31 left in the third quarter. During the previous 50 Super Bowls, no team had come back from a deficit larger than 10 points. Maybe this just wasn't the Patriots' day.

Then the Patriots, led by their defense and their quarterback, Tom Brady, began to mount a comeback. Two Patriots touchdowns and a field goal closed the gap to 28-20. The Falcons were quickly unraveling. Their lead had disappeared, sending the team into panic mode.

Meanwhile, Brady was on a mission. The Patriots' quarterback marched his team down the field in the final minutes. After a one-yard touchdown run by Josh White, Brady capped the comeback with a two-point conversion pass to Danny Amendola.

For the first time in NFL history, the Super Bowl was headed to overtime. Brady and the Pats received the ball first and shredded the Falcons defense with a 75-yard drive that ended with White scoring his third touchdown. The comeback was complete, and Brady was voted Super Bowl MVP for a record fourth time.

BEST!

Tom Brady

DENVER'S DEBACLE

From the beginning, it seemed that **Super Bowl XLVII**, which followed the 2013 season, was going to be a letdown for the **Denver Broncos**. On the Broncos' first snap, star quarterback Peyton Manning and his center had a miscommunication. Manning wasn't ready, and the ball sailed past Manning and resulted in a safety. The **Seattle Seahawks** added two field goals and a pair of touchdowns to go up 22-0 by halftime.

Any hopes of a Denver comeback were gone after the opening kickoff of the second half when Seattle's Percy Harvin returned the kick 87 yards for a TD. It was a deficit that not even Manning, the Broncos' legendary quarterback, could overcome. Denver lost by a final score of 43-8.

Tom Dempsey

DEMPSEY FROM DEEP!

KICKERS

Kickers who make clutch field goals can be the toast of the town. Kickers who miss might be better off leaving town.

THAT'S A FACT
Tom Dempsey held the record for longest field goal in league history for more than 40 years. Matt Prater of the Denver Broncos kicked a 64-yarder in 2013.

Though Tom Dempsey was born without his right toes and fingers on his right hand, he blossomed into an NFL kicker. Over an 11-year career, Dempsey did it his way. When most kickers began using a "soccer style" kicking approach that has become today's norm, Dempsey stayed with the straight-on style. He also wore a shoe that was modified to fit his foot.

In 1970 Dempsey entered the NFL record books. His New Orleans Saints were down by a point in the final seconds against Detroit. The Saints' final shot at winning the game would come on a 63-yard field goal attempt. Keep in mind that the record at the time for longest field goal was 56 yards. Dempsey wasn't fazed. He knocked the 63-yarder through the uprights, winning the game and breaking the previous record by seven yards.

A 47-yard field goal attempt is no easy task. Add a little pressure — say a kick for all the marbles. That's what Buffalo Bills kicker Scott Norwood was facing with eight seconds remaining in Super Bowl XXV and his team trailing the New York Giants, 20-19.

Norwood lined up to kick. The ball was snapped. Norwood's attempt looked good off his foot. It had plenty of distance. But slowly, painfully, Norwood's kick faded right. It missed going between the goalposts, and the Bills lost. But give the fans of Buffalo credit for being loyal and understanding. Norwood was welcomed home after his miss with a standing ovation at the parade held in the Bills' honor.

WIIIIIDE RIGHT

Scott Norwood

CHAPTER 3

Decisions & Collisions

COACHES

NEW ORLEANS GAMBLE

BEST!

In pro football, coaches rule. They blow the whistles, dole out playing time, call the plays, and make key choices when the game is on the line. Then the coaches have to live with their decisions — the good, the bad, and the ugly.

Sean Payton didn't coach his way to the Super Bowl without taking chances. But the play Payton called to start the second half of Super Bowl XLIV was risky. Very risky.

Payton's New Orleans Saints were trailing the Indianapolis Colts 10-6 at halftime. During the break, Payton huddled with his coaches and decided his team would go with their "ambush" play. The Saints' ambush play was an onside kick, which would hopefully catch Indy off-guard.

Adding to the degree of difficulty was that the Saints kicker, Thomas Morstead, was a rookie. But Morstead kicked the ball perfectly. When all the players were removed from the pileup, Saints safety Chris Reins emerged with the ball.

Payton's decision paid off as the Saints marched down the field and scored. The ambush play jumpstarted a momentum swing that brought New Orleans its first Super Bowl.

WORST!

The Seattle Seahawks were a few feet away from their second consecutive Super Bowl victory. With only 26 seconds remaining, they were losing to the New England Patriots, 28-24, but they had second-and-goal from the Patriots 1-yard line. They had bruising running back Marshawn Lynch in the backfield. Surely the Seahawks would play the odds and give the ball to Lynch. Right? Right?!

SLEEPLESS IN SEATTLE

Offensive coordinator Darrel Bevell had a different plan. Bevell called a passing play, and head coach Pete Carroll agreed. Quarterback Russell Wilson threw a quick slant to receiver Ricardo Lockette. But Patriots defensive back Malcom Butler saw the pass coming, and intercepted the ball.

Forget the Seahawks. All football fans were in disbelief. The Patriots ran out the clock for the win. The call cost Seattle the Super Bowl.

YOUTH MOVEMENT

In 2017 **Sean McVay** became the youngest head coach in NFL history when the Los Angeles Rams hired him at the age of 30. McVay was only about five years older than the average NFL player. Marv Levy and George Halas were the oldest head coaches in league history — both were 72 years old when they retired.

Sean McVay

19

TRADES

NFL teams make trades hoping to press the reset button. Trades can turn franchises' fortunes around . . . or send them into tailspins.

MARSHALL LAW

Marshall Faulk

FACT BREAK

The Miami Dolphins actually offered the Colts what was considered a better trade package for Marshall Faulk at the time. But Indianapolis didn't want to send Faulk to a team in the same division.

Sometimes, the best trades happen when neither team regrets the transaction. Marshall Faulk's trade from Indianapolis to St. Louis is a prime example.

Faulk was a star running back with the Colts. In 1998 he combined for more than 2,000 total rushing and receiving yards. But the Colts traded Faulk in 1999 to St. Louis. Faulk had his best rushing season yet and helped the Rams' "Greatest Show on Turf" offense win the Super Bowl in 1999. Indy, meanwhile, selected Edgerrin James to replace Faulk with one of the draft picks they received in the trade. James won rushing titles in his first two seasons as a Colt and was a Pro Bowl cornerstone for seven seasons in Indy.

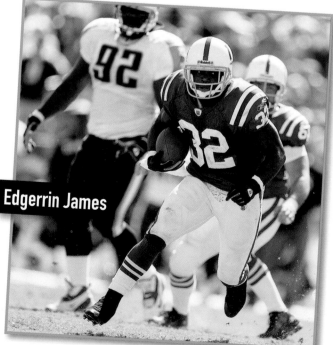

Edgerrin James

THE GREAT TRADE ROBBERY

Herschel Walker

An already talented Minnesota Vikings team hoped to reach the Super Bowl after trading for running back Herschel Walker in 1989. Instead, the "Great Trade Robbery" between Minnesota and Dallas handed the Cowboys a basket of draft picks that helped them lay the foundation for a Super Bowl dynasty in the 1990s.

In the largest trade in the NFL history, the Vikings shipped eight draft picks and five players to Dallas in exchange for Walker and four draft picks. Walker started off hot for Minnesota, rushing for 148 yards in his first game. But Walker never gained more than 1,000 yards for the team and was let go after the 1991 season.

In an odd twist of fate, Walker ended his career with Dallas, playing mostly as a kick returner.

DRAFT PICKS

Many teams build their talent pool through the NFL draft. If they look hard enough, legends can be found hiding in plain sight. But draft pick busts are even more common.

When the Patriots drafted Tom Brady in the sixth round of the 2000 Draft, Brady told Patriots owner Bob Kraft it was the best decision the franchise ever made. Brady's prediction couldn't have been more accurate. Brady has given New England five Super Bowl titles, set league records, and is arguably the greatest quarterback in league history. Not bad considering many sixth-round picks don't make the final roster.

SUPER STEALS

Antonio Brown

Antonio Brown was a standout player at Central Michigan University, but wasn't drafted until the Pittsburgh Steelers took a chance on him in the sixth round of the 2010 Draft. Pittsburgh's gain was the rest of the league's loss. Brown blossomed into the NFL's most dangerous receiver.

Russell Wilson was told he was too small to play NFL quarterback. But the Seattle Seahawks saw the possibilities in Wilson, drafting him in the third round of the 2012 Draft. In just his second year, Wilson became the face of the franchise and helped Seattle win in Super Bowl XLVIII.

Russell Wilson

Jamarcus Russell

Jamarcus Russell was supposed to save the Oakland Raiders when the team drafted the quarterback first overall in the 2007 NFL Draft. Russell's tenure with the team was a disaster, as he won only seven games over four seasons. After signing a contract paying $31.5 million, Russell was cut by the team in 2010.

BIG BUSTS

There was a heated debate before the 1998 NFL Draft: Who was the better quarterback, Peyton Manning or Ryan Leaf? The Indianapolis Colts chose Manning first. Leaf was drafted second by the San Diego Chargers. While Manning retired as the holder of many NFL records and two Super Bowl titles, Leaf was out of the league after just three seasons.

Ryan Leaf

SACKS

Quarterback sacks are when defensive players get their time to shine. This can be an excellent opportunity to show off dance skills. There are cautionary tales, though.

BEST!

LET'S DANCE

Von Miller

Denver Broncos linebacker **Von Miller** has averaged 12 sacks a season in the first six years of his career. He's imitated Superman, Forrest Gump, President Richard Nixon, and performed the "Funky Chicken." Miller's creative dances earned him a spot on "Dancing With the Stars."

The "Gangnam Style" dance craze showed up on the football field thanks to Cincinnati Bengals defensive tackle **Domata Penka**. After pouncing on Jaguars quarterback Blaine Gabbert, Penka stood up and started performing the dance phenomenon from South Korea. The 300-plus-pounder was surprisingly light on his feet.

THAT'S A FACT

The NFL didn't record sacks until 1982. Prior to declaring the behind-the-scrimmage tackle of the quarterback a "sack," the NFL called the play "dumping the passer."

BEST!

Clay Matthews

Clay Matthews has some huge biceps, and he's not afraid to show them off. When the Green Bay All-Pro linebacker sacks the quarterback, he crouches down, flexes his muscles, and howls.

SAD SACKS

WORST!

Stephen Tolloch learned the hard way it can be dangerous to mock another players' celebrations. In 2014 Tolloch was playing for the Detroit Lions when he sacked Green Bay quarterback Aaron Rodgers. Tolloch jumped in the air, and did his version of Rodgers' "championship belt" touchdown celebration. He landed and tore a ligament in his knee. His shenanigans cost him the rest for the season.

Celebrating when your team is losing by a large margin is never a good look. Chicago's **Lamar Houston** added injury to insult when he hurt himself celebrating a sack when his team was losing by 25 points. Houston leaped, fell, and missed the rest of the 2014 season.

END ZONE CELEBRATIONS

Some fans joke that the NFL stands for the "No Fun League." But touchdowns aren't easy to come by. That's why players like to take a moment to bask in end zone glory.

J.J. Watt

BEST!

DANCE FEVER

One of the simplest and best touchdown celebrations is the "Mile High Salute." Playing home games at Denver's Mile High Stadium inspired Broncos running back Terrell Davis to give many a sharp salute after scoring a sixer. J.J. Watt of the Houston Texans has made popular his own version of the salute.

The NFL outlawed players jumping into the crowd in 2000 — except at Green Bay's Lambeau Field. That's because that's where the "Lambeau Leap" started. One of the funniest celebrations still occurs when the occasional visiting player attempts his own Lambeu Leap. That usually ends up with him spit back out of the crowd.

LAMBEAU LEAP

THAT'S A FACT
In the mid-1960s, New York Giants receiver Homer Jones was the first known player to throw the football on the ground after a touchdown. He called the celebration a "spike."

OH, MY ACHING HEAD!

Gus Frerotte

Gus Frerotte was a respected journeyman quarterback. But the YouTube generation remembers Frerotte for one play. Frerotte's Washington Redskins were facing the New York Giants in 1997. Washington had the ball at the 1-yard line. Frerotte rolled to his right, saw daylight, and scampered to the end zone. Touchdown!

If only it would've ended there.

With no one in the immediate area to celebrate with, a pumped-up Frerotte ran toward a padded wall and head-butted it. When he jogged back to the sidelines, something didn't feel right. Turns out Frerotte had sprained his neck and couldn't finish the game.

CHAPTER 4

Fun & Fashion

BEST OF THE BEST

UNIFORMS

The NFL is a fashion forward league. Tradition sometimes meets head-on with innovative colors and designs. But when donning throwback jerseys, style can turn sour.

BEST!

The **Oakland Raiders**' silver and black never goes out of style. The colors are intimidating. Raiders gear also looks good off the field.

BEST!

The famous star seen on the helmet of the **Dallas Cowboys** is one of sports' most recognizable logos. The Cowboys also became the first team to start wearing their white jerseys at home. Most teams wear colored jerseys.

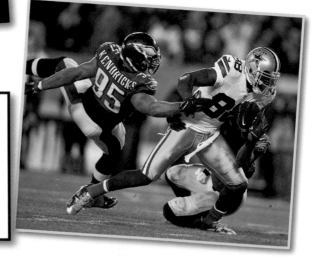

BEST!

Since the **Carolina Panthers** joined the NFL and began play in 1995, they've kept their uniform consistent. Owner Jerry Richardson says the team's uniforms won't change in his lifetime. The style and colors have remained the same: process blue, silver and black.

THROWBACK DISASTERS

WORST!

In recent years, teams began wearing throwback jerseys during select games. The **Green Bay Packers** throwback uniform dates back to the 1920s. What, couldn't they find matching colors back then? The navy blue isn't so bad. But matched with the yolk-hued helmets and tan pants. Uh . . . the Packers should stick with green and gold.

The **Pittsburgh Steelers** wore black-and-gold-striped throwback jerseys from the 1930s for several years in a row. Problem was, they looked more like bumblebees in jailhouse outfits than footballers. The team came to its senses and retired the bumblebee jerseys after the 2016 season. About time!

ABOUT THE AUTHOR

Drew Lyon's first magazine subscription was *Sports Illustrated for Kids*. He soon developed a lifelong love of reading and writing. He has been a freelance writer for more than 10 years and specializes in sports and culture pieces. He currently writes for *Minnesota Soybean Business Magazine*. Drew lives in Mankato, Minnesota, where he can often be found devouring biographies and crime novels.

GLOSSARY

blooper — an embarrassing public blunder

bust — a complete failure

onside kick — a kickoff in football in which the ball travels just far enough to be legally recoverable by the kicking team

scrimmage — the imaginary line in football separating the offense and the defense that may not be crossed until the football is hiked

rushing — the act of advancing a football by running plays

throwback — something suited to an earlier time or style

conversion — a successful attempt for a point or points after a touchdown

franchise — a team and its operating organization

cornerstone —a basic part of something; in sports, often used in reference to a player considered essential to a franchise

momentum — strength or force gained by motion or by a series of events

READ MORE

Bryant, Howard. *Legends: The Best Players, Games, and Teams in Football.* Puffin Books. 2016.

Martirano, Ron. *Football: Great Records, Weird Happenings, Odd Facts, Amazing Facts & Other Cool Stuff.* Imagine. 2015.

The Editors of Sports Illustrated for Kids. *Big Book of Who Football.* Sports Illustrated Kids Big Books. 2015.

INTERNET SITES

Use FactHound to find Internet sites related to this book.

Visit *www.facthound.com*

Just type in 9781543506143 and go.

INDEX